STEP-UP
RELIGION

How and why do Hindus and Sikhs celebrate Divali?

Jean Mead

Evans

Published by Evans Brothers Limited
2A Portman Mansions
Chiltern Street
London W1U 6NR

© Evans Brothers Limited 2008

Produced for Evans Brothers Limited by
White-Thomson Publishing Ltd,
Bridgewater Business Centre,
210 High Street,
Lewes, East Sussex BN7 2NH

Printed in China by New Era Printing Co. Ltd.

Project manager: Ruth Nason

Design and illustration: Helen Nelson at
Jet the Dog

British Library Cataloguing in Publication Data

Mead, Jean

How and why do Hindus and Sikhs celebrate
divali? - (Step-up religion)

1. Divali - Juvenile literature

I. Title

394.2'6545

ISBN-13: 9780237534127

Acknowledgements

Thanks are expressed to Sejal Patel, of Barnet Hill
Primary School, and Rashnita Patel, for advice on
the Hindu pages of this book; Narinder Matharoo
and the leaders of the Sikh Sangat, Leyton, for
their help with advice on the Sikh pages; and Janet
Monahan at the University of Hertfordshire for
advice on the teachers' page. The Author and
Publishers also thank the families of Sonal Patel
and Sumatiben Patel and of Mrs Bhanu, who were
willing to set up extra out-of-season Divali
celebrations for photographs in their homes.

Photographs are from: Alamy: cover tr, pages 16t
(ArkReligion.com), 19 (Photofusion Picture Library),
21 (ArkReligion.com), 22 (John Cole), 24l (Louise
Batalla Duran), 24c (Paul Doyle); Brent Cross
Shopping Centre: page 15b; Corbis: cover (main),
pages 17 (Arko Datta/Reuters), 20 (Raminder
Pal Singh/epa), 23b (Ajay Verma/Reuters);
Getty Images: pages 4 and 12 (AFP), 5 (AFP),
6b (Bushnell/Solfer), 7, 9 (AFP), 11 (AFP);
iStockphoto.com: cover tl, pages 1 (Ian Ferguson),
6tl (Elena Elisseeva), 6tr (Imad Birkholz), 14 (Frank
van den Bergh), 25t (Ken Sorrie); Jean Mead:
pages 8, 10, 13t, 16b, 18, 23t, 24r, 25b;
Topfoto/Image Works: page 13b; White-Thomson
Picture Library: page 27 (Chris Fairclough).

Contents

Divali is the Indian festival of light

Divali is a very popular festival, celebrated in October or November all over India and by Indian people around the world. The date of the festival is fixed according to the Hindu calendar, which is based on the cycle of the moon. Therefore, on the standard international calendar, the date varies a little from year to year. The festival is called the festival of light.

▲ Decorating houses and temples with rows of little clay lamps called divas, or other lights, is a beautiful and important part of Divali.

▼ *Divali began in India, but has spread around the world as Indian families have migrated to all the other countries labelled on this map.*

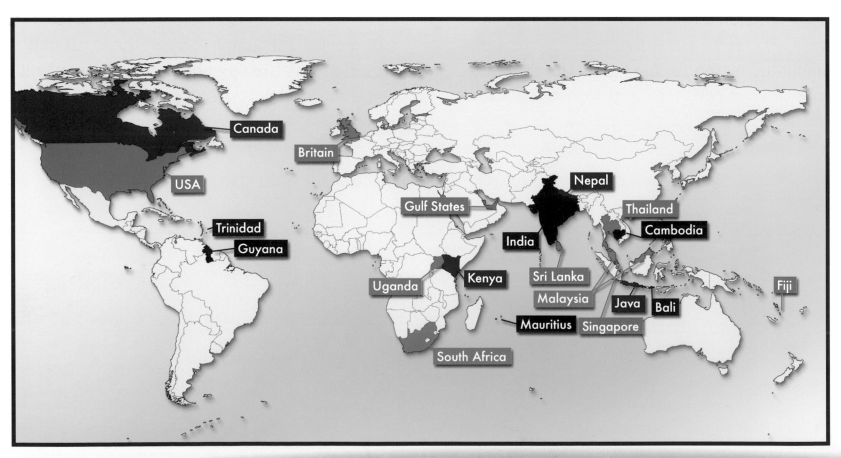

Canada
Britain
USA
Nepal
Gulf States
Thailand
Trinidad
Cambodia
Guyana
India
Kenya
Sri Lanka
Fiji
Uganda
Malaysia
Java
Bali
Mauritius
Singapore
South Africa

The name Divali comes from a Sanskrit word, 'Deepavali', meaning a row of lights. When the name is translated into English, it is sometimes written as 'Diwali' – with a 'w' instead of a 'v'. Either spelling can be used, because the sound in Sanskrit is half way between a V and a W.

Divali celebrations are full of excitement, light and colour, with fireworks, bright clothes and decorations, special food and family and community get-togethers. There are religious celebrations, and religious stories are told.

Differences

Everywhere that Divali is celebrated, people enjoy the light of the divas, and stories are told about the reason for the lights. But the stories and ways of celebrating are not all the same.

India is a huge country with different climates and calendars. People in different parts of India have their own languages, cultures and religions, with different gods being worshipped. Therefore their customs for celebrating Divali vary. In other countries, Indian people have developed their own ways of celebrating Divali, based on the traditions of the part of India from which they came.

Hindus and Sikhs

The two main religions in which Divali is celebrated are Hinduism and Sikhism. Hindus welcome different gods and goddesses on each of the five days of the festival. Sikhs sometimes call the festival 'Bandi Chhor Divas'. 'Bandi chhor' means 'freeing people from prison' and gives a clue about the story that Sikhs celebrate.

◀ A Hindu temple in Leicester is lit up for Divali. Britain has the largest population of Hindus and Sikhs outside India. Some famous and fantastic Divali celebrations take place in several British towns.

Celebrating light

We need light to see the world and each other, and to see to do things. We make lights that we can use to help us to see when it's dark, and to guide us at night, like runway lights for aeroplanes. Many people love light, whether it is sunlight, candlelight, electric light, or torchlight. Light can make us feel cheerful, warm and safe. Lights are a sign of welcome.

Because light makes us feel good, people often use light to make special occasions bright and beautiful. Celebrations are more exciting with bright lights, torchlight processions and fireworks.

▲ *When do people use fairy lights like these? What do they make you feel?*

▶ *Do you feel glad when the sun comes out from behind dark clouds?*

Light in religious celebrations

In religions all over the world, lights are used as a symbol to show joyful things. Several religions have festivals of light near the middle of winter. Why do you think they are especially popular at this time of year?

◀ *At the festival of Hanukkah, Jewish people light candles on eight nights. The festival remembers a story from Jewish history, in which the Jews got their temple back from their enemies, and the temple lamp kept burning for eight days even though the lamp oil had run out.*

At Easter, Christians remember the death of Jesus and then his coming back to life, called the Resurrection. At some churches people take part in a vigil, which begins in darkness to remember the sadness of Jesus's death. Then one candle is lit and its light is passed on until everyone is holding a lighted candle and the church is ablaze with light, as a symbol of joy in the belief that Jesus is alive again.

Light overcomes darkness

Darkness can be scary. Many people do not like the dark unless they know they are safe in bed. People who do bad things usually do not want others to see them, so they like darkness to hide in. When people come home to a dark house, the first thing they do is switch on the lights. It is wonderful how different we may feel when the light chases away the darkness.

Light overcoming darkness is often used as a symbol of good overcoming evil, or of knowledge overcoming ignorance. On the next four pages, you will find out about a Hindu story in which good finally overcomes evil.

Dark and light feelings

With a group of friends and a teacher or parent, sit for several minutes in a darkened room. Tell each other what feelings the darkness gives you. Then the grown-up can light a torch, diva or candle, and you can say how your feelings change. List words about dark and opposite words about light, and use these in a poem to show your feelings about light and dark.

A story that Hindus tell at Divali

At Divali Hindus celebrate the end part of a very long story from a sacred poem called the Ramayana. These two pages tell you how the story begins.

The Ramayana is about Rama and his wife Sita. Rama is an avatar of the god Vishnu. An avatar means a form in which a god or goddess appears on earth. Sita is an avatar of the goddess Lakshmi.

The exile of Rama

Once upon a time, in the Indian kingdom of Ayodya, Prince Rama was the oldest and much loved son of King Dasharatha. Rama married Sita, a beautiful princess.

Rama had a stepmother who wanted her son, Bharata, to be the next king, instead of Rama. She tricked Dasharatha into promising to banish Rama from the kingdom for 14 years.

King Dasharatha was sad but, to keep his promise, he sent Rama into exile.

Rama obeyed his father, and left for a forest land far away. Sita and Lakshman, Rama's loyal brother, went with him. They lived in a hut in a forest clearing, hunting and gathering food from the forest.

Whenever Rama and Lakshman went out hunting, they made a magic circle around the hut in which Sita would be safe.

◀ *In a shrine of a Hindu temple, statues and pictures of the gods and goddesses are called murtis. They are beautifully dressed and given garlands of flowers. These are murtis of Lakshman (left), Rama and Sita and the monkey god Hanuman.*

Sometimes people put on plays of the Ramayana story. This actor took part as the demon Ravana.

Image search

Find images of Rama, Sita and Hanuman on www.hindunet.org/hindu_pictures/ (click on 'gods and goddesses'). In some pictures, Rama is blue. This is a way of showing that he is an avatar of Vishnu.

Cut and paste suitable pictures into sequence to tell part of the Ramayana story. You may be able to show your work to the class on the interactive whiteboard.

The capture of Sita

Rama, Sita and Lakshman had an enemy, the ten-headed demon Ravana. He wanted to capture Sita.

One day a beautiful golden deer appeared in the forest. Rama and Lakshman chased it, but it was a trick. While Sita was alone, a poor-looking man came begging for food, and in her kindness she stepped outside the magic circle to give him something to eat. At once he changed into Ravana in his demon form, and snatched Sita away in his chariot in the sky. He took her to his island kingdom of Lanka.

Rama and Lakshman searched for Sita in despair. The monkey king, Hanuman, got his armies to help to look for her, and eventually a bird told him that Sita had been taken across the ocean to Ravana's island.

The power of evil

From the story so far, it looks as if evil has won. King Dasharatha was tricked. Rama was sent away. Sita was deceived and kidnapped by Ravana. Rama and Lakshman could not rescue her. It looks hopeless. We can see some good qualities, such as Rama's obedience to his father, Sita's and Lakshman's loyalty, and Hanuman's efforts to help, but they don't seem enough. What do you think might happen next?

What happens at the end of the story?

These two pages show how, at the end of the story, the good characters triumph over the evil ones.

▶ *There are many shortened versions of the Ramayana, and it is often told in comic books and videos. The details chosen for these shortened versions are not always the same.*

The rescue of Sita

Hanuman made a giant leap across the sea to Lanka. Sita was imprisoned there in a tower because she would not become Ravana's wife.

Hanuman found Sita, and showed her a ring that Rama had given him. He promised to fetch Rama to try to rescue her. Then Ravana's guards captured Hanuman and set the end of his tail on fire. He leapt from the window, ran through the town, setting fire to everything as he went, and escaped from the island.

When Hanuman told Rama and Lakshman what he had found, they raised a great army of monkeys, who built an enormous bridge of stones across to the island. In a battle with the armies of Ravana, many of the monkey army were killed or injured.

Hanuman saw that Rama was wounded and that Lakshman had been killed. Rama said that some magic herbs from a mountain in the Himalayas had the power to cure him and bring Lakshman back to life, so Hanuman sped off to find the herbs. As he didn't know which they were, he lifted the whole mountain and took it to Rama, to choose what he needed.

In a final face-to-face battle, Rama shot and killed Ravana with a golden arrow. Sita could now be rescued and reunited with Rama.

The welcome home

The joyful news spread through the country that Rama had won the battle and Sita had been rescued. Rama, Sita, Lakshman and Hanuman started the journey back to Ayodya. Rama's father, the king, had died, and his half-brother Bharata had put a pair of Rama's sandals on the throne to keep it for him when he returned.

Rama, Sita, Lakshman and Hanuman passed through many villages on their way home. People were delighted and decorated their villages, and put lights outside their houses to welcome Rama and Sita and guide their way.

▶ *A temple in the shape of Hanuman has been built in New Delhi, India. Hanuman is often shown with Rama's name or a picture of Rama and Sita in his heart, to represent his devotion to Rama. Hindus pray to Hanuman, 'You make all difficult tasks very easy. You possess the power of devotion to Rama.'*

What does the story mean?

The ending of the Ramayana gives people hope that, even when things seem impossibly hard, good can triumph. What other stories do you know in which good triumphs in the end? Can you think of an example from real life?

'Jigsaw' the story

In a group of five, take one character of the Ramayana story each. Research the part your character played and think about how he or she might feel. Then put the story back together: in your group, discuss what happened to each character and what each one learned.

How is the story celebrated at Divali?

Re-telling the story

The Ramayana story is told in different ways in different places. At Divali in India, Hindus celebrate the end of the story, when Rama and Sita return home joyfully. It is like the final part of a serial story, which is told over many months. In Britain, the whole story of Rama and Sita is often told at Divali.

Welcoming lights

Traditionally, in Indian villages with no street lights, people lit diva lamps to welcome visitors after dark. The little clay lamps, filled with ghee, were set on verandas and in doors and windows. If an important visitor was expected, the whole village would be lit up.

At Divali, many Hindus light their homes in this way, as a reminder of how villages welcomed Rama and Sita on their journey home to Ayodya. People use traditional divas and also decorate homes, shops, streets and temples with strings of multi-coloured lights.

▼ *Traditional divas are little 'thumb-pots' made of fragile, unbaked clay, so people buy new ones every year. Potters make thousands of them for the festival each year. Sometimes people paint patterns on them.*

Make a diva

Use clay or plasticine to make a diva, a thumb-pot with a small lip, large enough to hold a tea-light. Paint it with colourful patterns and when it is dry, coat it with PVA glue.

Remembering the gods and goddesses

In India, Divali lasts five days, but in Britain it is often squeezed mainly into a weekend. Traditionally, on each of the five days, Hindus remember different gods and goddesses for the parts that they played in the battle of good against evil. People welcome the deities into their homes and worship them at the household shrine. On the first day of Divali even Yama, the god of death, is honoured, when families light a single lamp so that the souls of their ancestors can return to visit them.

Friends and families get together at Divali. In India, where the weather is warm, the main festivities take place in homes and in the street. In Britain, the weather is colder and Hindu homes may be widely apart, and therefore many celebrations take place at temples or mandirs. The mandirs are beautifully lit and Hindus gather there for festival pujas, music and celebrations.

Hindu worship, called puja, includes offering flowers, food and light to the images of the deities. At this home shrine, one of the boys offers the aarti lamps and everybody sings.

▶ *Hindus take food to the temple or mandir to offer to the deities, and later everyone shares the food, which is believed to have been blessed by the deities. On one day of Divali called Annakuth (see page 17), lots of special food is piled in front of the murtis.*

Welcoming visitors

Cleaning

Many people expect lots of visitors at Divali, and part of preparing for them – especially if they include gods and goddesses – is to clean the house thoroughly. An extra reason for doing the cleaning is that the first day of Divali, called Naraka Chaturdasi, celebrates a story about the god Krishna, who fought the demon of filth. This story (below) of good triumphing over evil is popular in south and west India.

◀ *This figure on a Hindu temple in Singapore shows Krishna. He is coloured blue, to show that he is an avatar of Vishnu. In his right hand, he holds a wheel, called a chakra, with which he cut off Naraka's head.*

Krishna versus the demon of filth

Naraka, the demon king in Assam, was harassing good and pious people. There was much rejoicing when Krishna won a great battle against Naraka and finally, at daybreak, cut off his head. Krishna set free all the princesses whom Naraka had thrown into prison.

Before he died, Naraka begged Krishna's forgiveness. He also asked Krishna: 'May people who have a holy bath on this day every year be saved from all evils.'

Can you explain why people celebrate this story of Krishna and the demon of filth by having an early morning ceremonial bath, using sweet-smelling essences? They also wear new clothes and let off firecrackers.

Rangoli patterns

Lights make houses look welcoming at night. To make their homes beautiful and welcoming in the daytime too, people decorate them with rangoli patterns. Rangoli is a Gujarati word meaning a mixture of colours. The Bengali word is 'alpana'.

In India the patterns are traditionally made on the floor of verandas or outside, like laying down a red carpet for royalty. Rice flour and coloured spices were used at first, making 'edible/biodegradable art' which could be

▼ *Sometimes people make huge rangoli patterns in public places such as shopping centres. What designs have been used here?*

eaten by insects and birds. Nowadays mostly chalk or powder paint is used and the patterns are made on boards or card. Often people enter competitions for the best rangoli pattern, organised by their mandir or community centre.

▲ *Symmetrical designs and sacred Hindu symbols are used in rangoli patterns. The symbols often include a lotus flower for the goddess Lakshmi, or a swastika, which is an ancient symbol of welcome often found over the door of homes in India.*

Make a rangoli pattern

Design and make a rangoli pattern. You can find some traditional designs at www.diwalifestival.org/rangoli-patterns-design.html and at www.snaithprimary.eril.net/rang.htm. Draw your design on card or stiff paper. Paint it with PVA glue, and carefully use a paper-cone funnel to put coloured powder paint onto it.

Welcoming Lakshmi and Bali

◀ *People take sweets, presents and cards to those they work with, to wish them happy Divali. The large card here has a picture of the goddess Lakshmi. Can you see coins falling from one of her hands?*

▼ *This home shrine or mini-temple for Lakshmi is decorated with lights and offerings of fruit and sweets. Each Divali, special coins are offered to the goddess. On the plate is the collection of coins from previous years, which the children have washed, and some new ones.*

Lakshmi, the goddess of wealth and good fortune

The second day of Divali is celebrated as the birthday of the goddess Lakshmi, the wife of Vishnu. She is considered to be the goddess of wealth and good fortune, and so many people gamble on this day if they feel that Lakshmi is around! Families try to make their home particularly bright and welcoming to attract Lakshmi, hoping that a visit will bring good fortune. Each home has a shrine for Lakshmi.

◀ *At this business place in Bombay, divas are held while prayers are said at the beginning of the financial year.*

Bali, the king of the underworld

On the third day of Divali a surprising god is welcomed: Bali, the king of the underworld. This is the only day of the year that puja is offered to him. The story below explains why.

New Year day

In Gujarat, in west India, the second day of Divali is New Year day, called Annakuth. It is also the beginning of the financial year, when businesses try to have all their accounts settled and debts paid. Gujarati business people take their account books to a Lakshmi puja at the temple, to ask for Lakshmi's blessing.

Think about new beginnings

Talk to your family or class about how many 'new years' there are in a year. Are there other chances for new beginnings? How do they make you feel? Do you usually write especially neatly when you begin a new exercise book?

Why is there a day for welcoming Bali?

Bali, ruler of the underworld, extended his kingdom over the earth as well.

One day, Vishnu took the form of a dwarf Brahmin [priest] and asked Bali to grant him space the size of three of his steps. Bali agreed.

The Brahmin then grew into a giant. With one step, he covered the entire earth. With the second step, he covered the sky. So he asked Bali where he should put his third step. Bali had no choice but to show his own head.

Vishnu placed his foot on Bali's head, pushing him back to the underworld where he belonged.

However, Bali prayed to Vishnu to be permitted to visit the earth once each year. Vishnu granted this wish, and so people offer their respect to Bali on this one day.

Some more Hindu Divali customs

Clothes

Most Hindus buy or make new, colourful outfits for Divali. Men, who may wear western clothes for the rest of the year, often wear decorated waistcoats and traditional Indian trousers and tunics, called shalwar kameez, for Divali. Women wear beautiful saris, sometimes with gold embroidery or

◀ As well as wearing beautiful clothes, some women make their hands and feet pretty with decorative patterns called mendhi, made with henna paste.

▼ These Hindu children wear smart traditional Indian clothes for family parties at Divali.

tiny mirror decorations, and lots of bright jewellery. Honoured guests and images of the deities are given garlands of flowers to wear.

Festive food

If visitors are expected, families prepare feasts of curry and rice and snacks such as samosas, pakoras and poppadums. The food is presented beautifully, on best plates, often decorated with garlands. Rice dishes may even be decorated with real gold leaf on top.

▶ Sweet desserts are not eaten most of the year, so at Divali people really enjoy giving Indian sweets to each other.

Music and dancing

In mandirs and at family gatherings people love music and dancing. In one traditional Divali dance, the 'dandia raas', everyone has a stick, which they tap faster and faster against that of a partner. The noise of banging sticks is said to remind people of how the Hindu gods drove out evil from the world.

Brothers' day

The last day of Divali is Brothers' day, Bhai beej, which is a strong tradition in Gujarati families. It is a day for brothers and sisters to be together and value each other. Grown-up brothers travel to meet their sisters, who cook them a special meal. The sister performs an aarti puja for her brother and puts a red powder mark called a tilak on his forehead. Brothers give their sisters presents or money and promise to protect them.

Firework displays

Divali days usually end with spectacular firework displays. These are a reminder of the story of Rama and Sita. Do you remember what happened after Ravana set fire to Hanuman's tail?

▲ Like other Divali customs, the stick dance called the 'dandia raas' adds to the feeling of joy and helps people to remember and celebrate the victory of good forces over evil ones.

Talk to a Hindu visitor

It may be possible for a Hindu visitor to come to your school, to talk about Divali and show pictures, clothing and artefacts. What would you like them to show you? What are three questions that you would ask?

A story that Sikhs tell at Divali

The Sikh religion began about 500 years ago in the Punjab region of northern India. Sikhs worship one God. They tell stories of ten Gurus, who were teachers and leaders in the first two hundred years of the religion.

Sikhs celebrate Divali in some similar ways to Hindus, but the story that they remember at the festival is a different one. It is a story about Guru Har Gobind, who was the sixth Sikh Guru from 1606 to 1644.

What does the story mean?

Read the story on page 21. Then, with a group if possible, re-tell it, thinking about what each character did and why. Finish the sentences:

- I think this story means ...

- I think it might encourage Sikhs to ...

▶ *The Golden Temple in Amritsar is the most important place of worship for Sikhs. It was built in the time of the fifth Sikh Guru, Guru Arjan Dev. At Divali it is lit up, and divas are floated in the huge pool of holy water that surrounds it.*

The princes and the Guru's cloak

In the 17th century, northern India was part of the Mogul empire. The Moguls were Muslims and, at this time, they were in conflict with Hindus and wanted to stop the Sikh religion from growing. The Mogul rulers had ordered Guru Har Gobind's father to be tortured to death, and they were afraid that Guru Har Gobind was plotting revenge.

However, the Mogul emperor Jehangir respected Guru Har Gobind and admired his holiness. This made the emperor's advisors suspicious and jealous and they wanted to keep Guru Har Gobind away. They persuaded Jehangir to keep him captive in Gwalior fort.

At the fort, Guru Har Gobind was treated well and spent his time in prayer, but he met many Hindu princes imprisoned there, who were starving and in rags. The Guru tried to help the Hindu prisoners, sharing his food and getting proper clothes for them.

Many people protested and asked Jehangir to release the Guru, but the emperor fell ill and forgot about him for two years. When he was well again, he remembered, realised that he

Guru Har Gobind is regarded as a saint and a soldier. He carried two swords, symbolising spiritual power and worldly power, which have become part of the Sikh symbol called the khanda.

had been wrong and sent orders to release Guru Har Gobind. However, the Guru refused to leave the fort unless the Hindu princes were also released. The emperor grudgingly agreed, saying, 'Let those princes be freed who can hold on to the Guru's cloak and walk out of prison with him.'

The prison gate was through a narrow passage, and Jehangir thought that only four or five would be able to squeeze through with the Guru. However, the Guru asked for a coat to be made with 52 long tassels, and so all the 52 Hindu princes could hold on to it and be freed.

Guru Har Gobind became known as 'Bandi Chhor' (one who frees people from prison). He arrived home at Amritsar on Divali day and the Golden Temple was lit with hundreds of lamps to welcome him. His mother ordered sweets and food to be given out, so that everyone could share a feast in celebration.

Why and how do Sikhs celebrate Divali?

How did the Sikh festival begin?

The Sikh religion grew up in Punjab, where people had been following Hindu beliefs and practices for many hundreds of years. Sikhs must have seen the Hindu Divali celebrations all around them. They did not want to worship the Hindu gods, but they liked the lights, festivities and fireworks.

The fourth Sikh Guru made the town of Amritsar a centre for the religion, and Sikhs began to gather there to receive blessings from their Guru. In 1619, at Divali time, the Golden Temple was illuminated to welcome Guru Har Gobind on his return from Gwalior fort. From then on, that day became a day of celebration for Sikhs. They call it 'Bandi Chhor Divas', which means 'Prisoners' release day'.

At the gurdwara

If they can, Sikhs visit the Golden Temple, which is lit inside and out with thousands of divas and electric lights (see the picture on page 20). If they can't get to Amritsar, they gather to worship and celebrate at their local gurdwara. Gurdwaras are decorated with lights, and worshippers take sweets and food to share. At the end of the evening, there are bonfires and fireworks.

▲ *Sharing is an important part of being a Sikh and so everyone who goes to the gurdwara, whatever their religion, is given free food in the kitchen called the langar. This happens every week, not just at Divali. In Indian culture, eating together is a sign of equality, and so the langar shows the Sikh belief that all people are equal. How is this belief shown in the story of Guru Har Gobind?*

Sikh worship is reading the holy book called the Guru Granth Sahib, singing hymns, and praying to the one God, whom Sikhs call 'Wahe Guru'. It means 'wonderful lord'. At Divali, the hymns are about how Guru Har Gobind fought for freedom and equality.

◀ *Some Sikhs send Divali cards with pictures of divas or a Guru. This card shows the first Guru, Guru Nanak.*

At home

Sikhs celebrate Divali at home, with best clothes, special food, visitors, lights, decorations and fireworks. Some families display a model of the Golden Temple, and sometimes people perform plays about the story of Guru Har Gobind. However, Divali is not the most important festival in the year for Sikhs. Can you find out which is their most important festival?

Web quest

List things you would like to know about Sikhs, and do a 'web quest'. Some Sikh websites are www.sikhs.org, www.sikhnet.com, www.sgpc.net, www.allaboutsikhs.com, and www.sikhpoint.com. Look for clues about what is important to Sikhs.

▶ *Sikhs in the northern Indian city of Chandigarh light diva lamps at a public ceremony for peace organised by the Anti-Terrorist Front of India. Sikhs and Hindus joined together at Divali, lighting lamps to symbolise unity in fighting for freedom from terrorism, and the victory of good over evil.*

Similar but not the same

The Sikh festival of Divali began in a place where Hindu Divali traditions were already well-known. Also, the event that Sikhs remember at their festival happened exactly at the time of Hindu Divali. Therefore, Sikh and Hindu Divali celebrations are similar. However, they are not the same. Which religion do you think these children belong to?

A Venn diagram

Use ICT to draw two overlapping circles, one called Hindu Divali, the other Sikh Divali. In the overlapping section write things that are the same for Hindus and Sikhs at Divali. Write things that are different in the other parts of the circles.

Divali is exciting with all the bright lights and fireworks, and the divas are beautiful. We love eating so many sweets!

At the gurdwara we hear the story of Guru Har Gobind. It's inspiring because he saved the princes even though they weren't from his religion. He taught that God wants us to fight for justice for everybody.

We do pujas for many gods and goddesses but my favourite is Lakshmi, because I hope she brings me luck. I like Hanuman too: he's like a super-hero in the Rama story.

Why are the Hindu and Sikh festivals different?

The descriptions below show how the Hindu and Sikh religions are different from each other. Which parts of these descriptions help you to understand the differences between Hindu Divali and Sikh Divali?

▲ *The Hindu god Hanuman is shown holding a mountain and a club. Can you say why?*

Hinduism

The word 'Hinduism' describes a mixture of religions that grew out of prehistoric religions in the Indus valley. Hinduism includes worship of many gods and goddesses and there is great variety, with different Hindus having different customs. Hindu stories are ancient myths about gods and goddesses from many scriptures. The gods and goddesses are magical and supernatural, but they may have qualities that Hindus admire. Although there are different Hindu ideas about how it all fits together, all Hindu worship involves individuals and priests offering devotion and puja to various murtis.

Sikhism

The word 'Sikh' means disciple. Sikhism began in the Punjab area when people became disciples of ten Gurus who taught people to worship the one God. The Gurus created a united community instead of different castes, and taught the importance of everybody being equal. Sikh stories are of human Gurus fighting for what they believed in and defending the new community. Sikh worship involves everyone reading from the Guru Granth Sahib, singing hymns in praise of God and praying, and it always includes eating together. Sikhism is a very practical religion, which places great importance on hard work, sharing and equality, and remembering God.

► *In this picture of the ten Sikh Gurus, Guru Har Gobind is in the top right corner. Do you remember the name of the first Guru, who is shown in the centre?*

So why are festivals important?

By looking at the festival of Divali as it is celebrated in two different religions, we can work out some of the things that are important in any religious festival. Think about a religious or non-religious festival that you celebrate. Does it have all of the same types of 'ingredients'? Think about how a festival is different from other sorts of celebrations such as birthdays. Is a solemn commemoration like Remembrance Day a 'festival of remembrance'?

▼ *Is it true that festivals always have the ingredients shown on this concept map?*

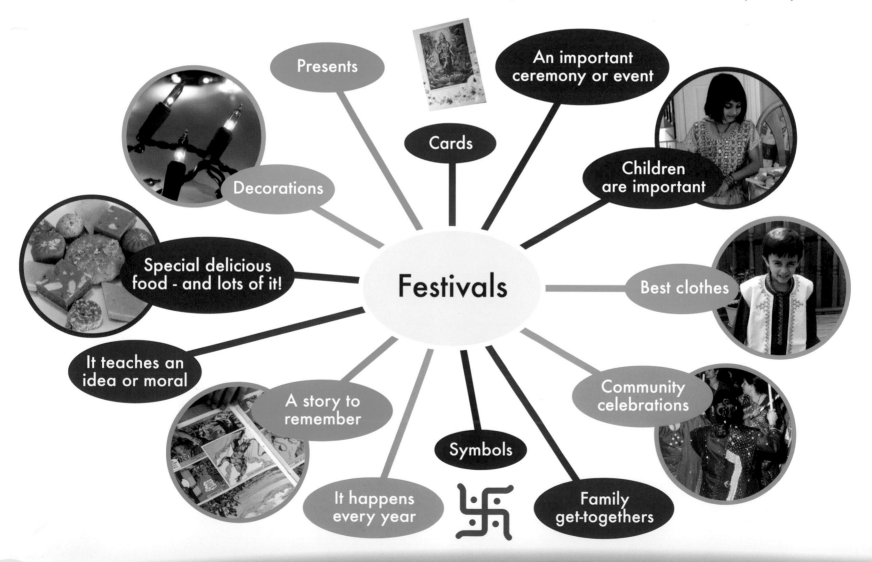

Presents

Cards

An important ceremony or event

Decorations

Children are important

Special delicious food – and lots of it!

Festivals

Best clothes

It teaches an idea or moral

A story to remember

Community celebrations

Symbols

It happens every year

Family get-togethers

Festival feelings

Whatever the festival, it is likely to give people the same sort of feelings, such as:

- I belong. It's good to meet everyone.

- I'm proud – I can celebrate what is important.

- I like to hear the old stories. It makes sure that they don't get forgotten.

- It reminds me of what is important and worth making a special effort for.

- It helps me to understand the symbols and meaning.

- It gives me something to look forward to, and something to remember afterwards.

▲ *Think of other festivals, such as Passover (above) and Christmas (below). Which ingredients from the festivals concept map do they have?* ▼

My favourite festival

Make a concept map of your own favourite festival. Use ICT and print it, and draw pictures to illustrate it. What do you like best about the festival?

27

Glossary

aarti — offering light to a deity, in Hindu worship. Ghee lamps are moved in circles in front of the image of the deity.

Annakuth — 'mountain of food' offered to the deities on New Year day in Divali.

avatar — the appearance of a Hindu deity in the form of a human or animal.

Bandi Chhor Divas — the name of the Sikh Divali festival. It means 'Prisoners' release day'.

Bengali — the language of the people of Bangladesh and West Bengal in India.

Bhai beej — a day for honouring brothers at Divali. Bhai means 'brother'.

ceremonial — done as a ceremony, a set action with a particular meaning.

castes — social groups into which Hindu society was divided.

chakra — a wheel-shaped weapon.

Christmas — the festival when Christians remember and celebrate the birth of Jesus.

commemoration — an event held in order for people to remember something or someone.

culture — the ideas and values of a society.

deity — a god or a goddess.

demon — an evil supernatural being.

devotion — love for someone that makes you give time and energy to serve them.

disciple — a follower, or learner.

diva — an oil lamp, traditionally made of clay, used at Divali and in Hindu worship.

Easter — the spring festival when Christians especially remember the death and resurrection of Jesus.

exile — being made to stay away from your own country or home.

financial year — for businesses, the twelve-month period at the end of which their accounts must be put in order.

garland — a necklace of flowers, given as a sign of honour.

ghee — clarified butter, especially used in Indian cooking or in lamps.

Gujarati — the language of the people of Gujarat in India.

gurdwara — a Sikh place of worship. Literally, it means 'the door of the Guru'.

Guru — teacher. In Sikhism, a Guru (with a capital G) means one of the ten leaders who founded the religion.

Guru Granth Sahib — the name of the Sikh holy book

Hanukkah — the eight-day Jewish festival of light, celebrated in November or December.

henna — a strong dye made from the leaves of a henna plant.

Hindu	relating to the religion of Hinduism, the ancient religion of India.
hymn	a song of praise to God.
khanda	the Sikh emblem, consisting of a doubled-edged sword surrounded by a circle and two curved swords.
langar	the free community meal served after services at a gurdwara, and also the kitchen/dining room in which the meal is served.
lotus flower	the large flower of the lotus plant, often associated with Lakshmi.
mandir	a Hindu temple or place of worship.
mendhi	henna paste used to make decorative designs on the hands and feet of Hindu, Sikh and Muslim women for festivals and celebrations.
Mogul empire	an important Muslim state which spread its rule across a large part of India in the 17th century.
murti	an image of a Hindu deity which is worshipped.
Naraka Chaturdasi	the day before the main day of Divali, on which Hindus celebrate Krishna's victory over the demon Naraka.
Passover	the spring festival when Jewish people remember how they escaped from slavery in Egypt.
puja	Hindu worship.
Ramayana	a great epic Sanskrit poem of Hinduism, telling the adventures of Rama.

rangoli	colourful patterns made with powder, traditionally on the floor, at Divali.
Resurrection	the coming back to life of Jesus after his death.
sacred	holy, to do with a god or religious worship.
Sanskrit	the language of ancient India, now only used in Hindu worship.
sari	traditional women's outfit in India; a length of cloth worn wrapped around the waist and draped over the shoulder.
shalwar kameez	traditional Indian or Pakistani outfit of loose trousers and tunic.
shrine	(in Hinduism) a place to worship a deity, in a temple or a home.
soul	the spiritual part of a human being which is believed to continue to exist after the body dies.
swastika	in Hinduism, a symbol of welcome, formed by a cross with the arms bent. (It was later adopted as a Nazi symbol.)
symbol	usually a picture or design that stands for something else.
temple	a place of worship. The word is used in several religions. Hindus use both 'temple' and 'mandir'. Sikhs use both 'temple' and 'gurdwara'.
tilak	a mark put on Hindus' foreheads to show that they have worshipped.
vigil	a time of praying or watching through the night, especially on the eve of a holy day.

For teachers and parents

This book has been designed to support and extend the learning objectives of Unit 3B of the QCA Religious Education Scheme of Work 'How and why do Hindus celebrate Divali?' and the new Year 4 unit 'How and why do people celebrate religious festivals? Hinduism and Sikhism'. It aims to encourage teachers and pupils to extend their understanding of the Hindu festival of Divali beyond the usual Rama and Sita story, by looking at the practices of each day of the festival, and the myths to which they are linked, in a way that shows some of the rich diversity within Hinduism. It also includes a section on Sikh Divali, which is less commonly recognised in schools. It engages children in thinking about the significance of Divali stories and practices for Hindus and Sikhs, both in participating in festivities and in learning how their values are influenced by stories in their religious heritage. It challenges children to explore the similarities and differences between the Hindu and Sikh Divali festivals, and links these to the underlying differences between the two religions. It can help contribute to 'Learning from religion' (RE Attainment Target 2) in that it looks at the significance of light in festivals and in people's emotions, explores the universal concept of good triumphing over evil, and analyses the key features of festivals, which all help pupils to relate their understanding to their own experiences. This helps meet the learning objectives 1a, 1b, 1c, 1d, 1e, 1f, 1g, 1h, and 2a, 2b, 2c, 2d, the themes 3e, 3f, 3g, 3i, 3j, 3l, and the experiences and opportunities 3o, 3p, 3q, 3s for Key stage 2 in the QCA Non-statutory National Framework for RE as they relate to two religions which feature in most Agreed Syllabuses.

FURTHER INFORMATION AND ACTIVITIES

Pages 4-5 Divali is the Indian festival of light

Be aware of diversity within religions. Pupils may well say, 'We don't do it that way, miss/sir!' Use a map to compare India – its size and geographical variety – to Britain, and point out the various regions as they are mentioned.

www.diwalifestival.org has a section on regional variations of Divali.

Counter stereotypes by making it explicit that not all Indians are Hindus. If there are Hindu and Sikh families in the school, ask them to show their geographical origins on the map, and identify which of the customs described in the book they follow. Jains also celebrate Divali but tell a story about the enlightenment of the Mahavira.

The date of Divali can be found on REonline >festivals calendar. Near Divali time look for coverage in the media and shops, especially where there are Hindu and Sikh populations, and make a display.

Plan a post-Divali assembly or party for the class.

Pages 6-7 Celebrating light

This page is a good opportunity for emphasis on inclusion. Links can be made to other religions that use light. Be careful not to make equivalences, such as 'Divali is their Christmas', but to explore the underlying common theme and symbolism of light. Darkness can symbolise evil or ignorance. From the Christian use of light, in Advent rings, baptismal candles, christingles and paschal candles, discuss what Jesus meant by 'I am the light of the world'. In Judaism, both the eternal light (ner tamid) in the synagogue and the hanukiah represent the menorah that symbolised God's presence in the Temple in Jerusalem.

Sikhs regard darkness as symbolising ignorance; and the coming of Guru Nanak as when 'ignorance has vanished, with light emerging over the world'.

The emotional aspects of light are something that all children can relate to and enjoy, and can provide opportunities for expressive writing and art. Ask the children to share their ideas about light and dark. Be sensitive about children's fears of the dark.

Make cross-curricular links to the science topic of light.

Check health and safety rules before using a candle or diva in class.

Pages 8-9 A story that Hindus tell at Divali

Krishna and Rama are two of the ten avatars or incarnations of the Hindu god Vishnu, who is said to have declared, 'When righteousness is weak and faints and unrighteousness exults in pride, then my spirit rises on earth, for the salvation of those who are good, for the destruction of evil in men, I come to this world.' (Bhagavad Gita IV: 6-9)

Many versions of the story can be found online or in books. A fuller version is in The Divali Story by Anita Ganeri (Evans). http://home.freeuk.net/elloughton13/dday.htm has five chapters of the longer story simplified from the Ramayana. Fuller exploration of the story could focus on the issues of relationships between all the characters.

http://hindunet.org/festivals/deevali/ and http://www.hindunet.org/god/Gods/index.htm have links to aspects of the festival.

Ram and Rama are alternative transliterations into English, and similarly for other words where the final 'a' is not written but included in the preceding consonant in Devanagri script.

A simple circle action song of the story suitable for younger children is on http://homepage.ntlworld.com/jeanmead/re/RE/Sita%20Song.html. The story can be dramatised, but some Sikh, Muslim, Jewish and Christian families may be unhappy about children portraying Hindu gods and goddesses. Puppets may be a preferable medium.

Pages 10-11 What happens at the end of the story?
www.hindunet.org/god/Gods/hanuman >images from darshan has images of Hanuman which can be matched to details of the story.

The 'jigsaw' activity can be used with a whole class. Each group investigates one character. Then children go back to 'story groups' to make a complete 'jigsaw' of the story.

Make a zig-zag-book 'comic strip' by folding a sheet of paper in half lengthways, then into four. On the four squares on one side draw four sad stages of the story (from pages 8-9), with speech bubbles. On the other side draw four pictures of the end of the story (pages 10-11).

Identify stories in books, films, TV, news, where good defeats evil, or ask children to think of stories in their own experience. Talk about how such stories make people feel and why.

Pages 12-13 How is the story celebrated at Divali?
Talk about how royalty or other VIP visitors might be welcomed, what decorations and preparations would be made and the excitement of anticipation. Perhaps invite a real VIP to school and involve the children in preparations – designing and making decorations, food, etc.

www.festivals.iloveindia.com/diwali and the BBC website have recipes for Divali food.

Use artefacts of puja-tray items to describe Hindu worship, along with a video extract. Avoid involving children in worship inappropriately.

Pages 14-15 Welcoming visitors
If you are inviting a visitor, let the children 'spring clean' the classroom.

http://www.snaithprimary.eril.net/rang.htm has some simple DIY rangoli patterns and links to more information and examples. Symmetrical rangoli patterns, made on a square divided into 16, can be linked to symmetry in maths. Easier than using paint to make a rangoli pattern is to stick on coloured foods, such as lentils and pasta. This is less traditional but is biodegradable.

The swastika often causes comment because it is familiar in its Nazi use. It is not true that Hitler 'reversed' the ancient Hindu symbol, as it is found in both directions in Hinduism.

Pages 16-17 Welcoming Lakshmi and Bali
Design and make Divali cards with pictures of divas or Lakshmi. See http://www.hindunet.org/hindu_pictures/GodandGoddesses/lakshmi.

www.123diwali.com has free animated/musical Divali cards. The fireworks ones are especially fun.

Pages 18-19 Some more Hindu Divali customs
Women of any religion in the Indian sub-continent decorate their hands for festivals and special occasions. A willing adult volunteer may have her hands decorated but it is not wise to allow children to do so. Outlines of hand shapes may be decorated with felt-tipped pens.

Gujaratis have a nine-night festival, Navaratri, in which dandia raas are specially danced, but such 'stick dances' feature at Divali too. You can make up a dance with two circles of dancers banging decorated sticks in a pattern. (Hand clapping with partners is less dangerous!)

In art, make firework pictures on black paper, using sparkle or sequins.

Pages 20-21 A story that Sikhs tell at Divali
www.allaboutsikhs.com >Sikh way of life>festivals>bandi chhor divas has a fuller version of the story.

Investigate the khanda symbol. The militant nature of Sikh symbols can raise difficult issues. It reflects the Sikhs' history as a persecuted minority. Children can discuss the importance of standing up for what is right, and protecting the weak.

Pages 22-23 Why and how do Sikhs celebrate Divali?
Divali celebrations in Sikh homes are often part of the Indian cultural background, while leaders at gurdwaras try to focus on the religious significance of the story of Guru Har Gobind and prefer to call the festival 'Bandi Chhor Divas'. Discuss with children diversity within religions and the spectrum of religious and cultural allegiance. Relate this to their own experiences of the range within any religious 'label'.

Ask for examples of occasions when children eat with family, friends or community, and discuss the emotional and social power of sharing food.

Pages 24-25 Similar but not the same
The ability to discern the underlying differences between superficially similar practices is important in growing maturity in RE. This page also helps children to make sense of specific religious features, such as a festival, by seeing them in the context of the whole religion. Review other aspects of the religions the children have encountered in RE and try to get a coherent overview.

Ask the children to write speech bubbles, saying what they enjoy about a festival they celebrate, without naming it. Then let the class sort them into 'sets' and discuss areas of overlap and distinctiveness.

In the picture on page 24 (right), one boy is dressed up as Krishna.

Pages 26-27 So why are festivals important?
List various secular, social or religious events and let the children use the concept map to analyse and decide which can be called 'festivals'.

Ask the children to produce a picture or collage or poem that conveys their feelings about a festival they celebrate.

Be aware that Jehovah's Witnesses do not mark special days like birthdays or festivals, but regard every day as equally holy.

USEFUL WEBSITES

www.qca.org.uk >I am interested in>subjects>Religious Education> Useful resources

www.diwalifestival.org

www.bbc.co.uk/leicester/faith/diwali/

www.festivals.iloveindia.com/festival

www.sikhiwiki.org

Index